**Renovating Silver,
Pewter and Brass**

Contents

D0236368

Introduction

Collecting and restoring old objects is becoming more interesting to many people, and this book covers some of the techniques of renovating items made in silver, pewter and brass. Although many repair jobs require major skills and specialist equipment, with guidance, knowledge, and some skill, the novice can renovate the battered pot or broken spoon so that it becomes once again a desirable, attractive object. Market stalls, sale-rooms and antique shops often have broken or damaged pieces lying in odd boxes which can often be bought quite cheaply. Even if beyond repair they are worth collecting to use as spares when renovating other things. Occasionally handles, knobs and legs are missing or broken, and a spare part from an irreparable object can sometimes be fitted, with perhaps some modification to make it harmonize with the piece being renovated. Worn out pieces of pewter and britannia metal are worth collecting, simply for the purpose of using them as solder to repair other pewter objects, or as raw material for casting new components. Similarly, silver objects which are worn out may be melted down to cast new parts.

Objects requiring renovation may range from large brass log boxes and pewter tankards to small pieces of

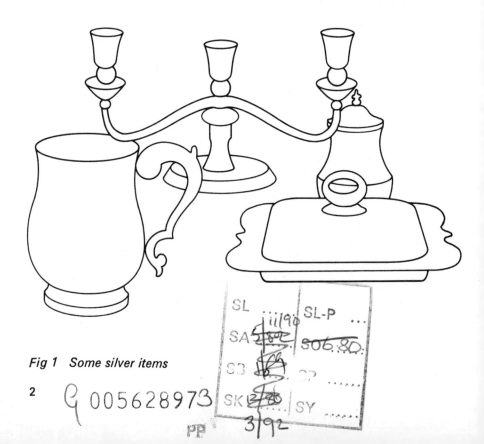

Fig 1   Some silver items

silver jewellery. Whatever the size of the object the approach to renovation should have a well-planned sequence. Before any of the renovation techniques described in this book are used, it is important to be able to identify silver, pewter and brass. While it is easy to differentiate between them because of their distinctive colours, it is much more difficult to differentiate between silver, silver plate and Sheffield plate. The novice could easily confuse a fine piece of Sheffield plate with a piece of silver and try to solder it, with disastrous results. Sheffield plate was constructed with tin solder, and would fall to pieces if subjected to the high temperatures required for silver solder. For centuries, pewter has been made in varying proportions of tin and lead, culminating in britannia metal and modern pewter which contain no lead. Frequently britannia metal is silver-plated and could be accepted as silver if marks are not closely examined and underlying metal exposed by scraping. The term 'brass' embraces a large number of alloys containing copper and zinc, from bronze to common yellow brass. Occasionally these alloys are silver-plated and on rare occasions gold-plated, so careful scrutiny is required. Although some guidelines are given, familiarity through handling and study is essential, and further reading as suggested by the bibliography is most important.

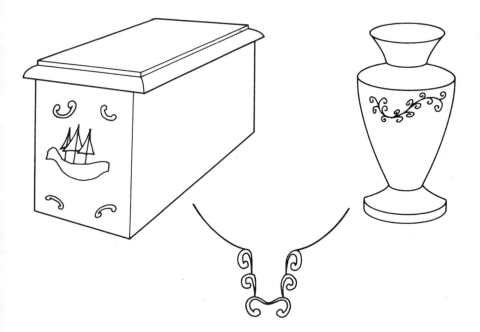

Fig 2   Some brass items

The metals and the methods used to identify them

Silver

A fine, ductile and malleable metal, with a perfect metallic lustre which is one of its distinctive features. It is one of the best-known conductors of electricity and heat. This latter property soon reveals itself to the renovator when soldering, for the heat from the soldering torch is quickly transmitted through the object. Silver objects which have been made in the United Kingdom are usually hallmarked. The hallmark is stamped by an Assay Office whose job it is to take a sample scraping from the object and test its silver content. There are two recognised qualities, namely Sterling – 92.5 per cent and Britannia – 95.84 per cent. Figure 1 shows a hallmark which gives the following information: the mark of the manufacturer, the quality of the silver alloy, the mark of the Assay Office, and the date letter. There are books available which give further information about hallmarks and date letter tables which are available from Assay Offices (see page 47).

If the object is not hallmarked, identification of the metal is more difficult. A piece may be found with the mark 800, which is a continental mark for silver alloy of 80 per cent silver content. Sometimes only the name 'Sterling' or 'Silver' is stamped. These marks cannot be taken as proof of the identity of the metal, so careful examination and the following chemical test should be made.

Make the following solution:

10gms sodium dichromate
25ml concentrated nitric acid
100ml water

The sodium dichromate is dissolved in some of the water; it will not dissolve in the acid. Add the acid to

Fig 3   Testing metal by scraping

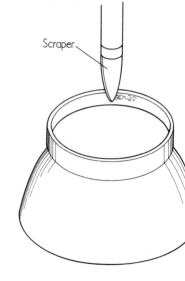

Scraper

4

Fig 5   A silver hallmark

Fig 6   EPNS mark

Fig 4   Features of Sheffield plate

the remainder of the water and then add the dissolved sodium dichromate. BUT *never add the water to the acid, always add the acid to the water*. Adding water to acid causes a violent reaction which is dangerous. Rubber gloves should be worn when handling the acid. This, and a range of solutions to test other metals, can be purchased from suppliers. Scrape a part of the object which is not visible as in Figure 3, such as the bottom of a foot or the inside of a base rim. The scraping must be sufficiently deep to prove that the object is not silver-plated base metal. When a drop of the solution is placed on a piece of silver, the spot will turn red immediately. The purer the alloy, the quicker the colour change and the deeper the red. If there is no colour change then the metal is not silver.

Silver plate and Sheffield plate

Objects which are electro-plated are usually so marked. The letters EPNS on an object mean electro-plated nickel silver, but beware, occasionally the letters are done in Old English lettering which can make the mark appear to be a Sterling silver hallmark. Sheffield plate was produced until about 1840 when electro-plating was invented. The principle of the method was to fuse silver on to copper using intense heat. The proportion of silver to copper was about one-tenth of the total thickness. The laminated billet produced was then rolled into a sheet. Early Sheffield plate had silver on one side only, so is easily identified, because the unplated side was simply tinned, but pieces made later, with silver coatings on both sides, are sometimes very difficult to identify. The secret is to examine edges and decorative applied parts with a magnifying glass, because they are attached with tin solder which makes a greyish line round the join. The edges of the open laminate always have a capping strip to conceal the copper core. There are touch marks peculiar to Sheffield plate, and specialist books are available on the subject (see page 48).

5

The metals and the methods used to identify them

Pewter

This word is probably derived from the old English word 'spelter' and is applied as a general name for a number of alloys, all of which contain tin in diverse proportions. This is best illustrated by explaining a little of its historical development.

Roman pewter, the oldest known, was composed of tin and lead, but occasionally with some traces of iron which are believed to have been accidentally introduced. There seem to have been two alloys in use : (a) 71·5 parts tin to 28·5 parts lead; (b) 78·2 parts tin to 21·8 parts lead. Continental pewter has a considerable history. 1437 Montpelier pewter was 96 parts tin to 4 parts lead for dishes and porringers, and 90 parts tin to 10 parts lead for salt cellars and ewers. Limoges used 100 parts tin to 4 parts lead. In 1576 Nuremburg pewter was 10 parts tin to 1 part lead. In France in the eighteenth century, the legal limit for lead content was 15 per cent, later 16·5 per cent with a 1·5 per cent margin for error, and this alloy was considered safe for the storage of wines.

English pewter, like silver, was controlled by legislation from very early times, no doubt because of the strength of the Pewterers' Guilds which were established in various towns. A brief history of the development of English pewter may be of interest. The first ordinances known are those of the London Guild dated 1348 which state that the alloy for rounded vessels should be 26lb of

Fig 7   Pewter touch mark

lead to every 1cwt of tin. A formula apparently exclusive to English ware which may have given it the reputation of superiority was called 'Fyne peauter'. The recorded formula states, 'as much brass as tin as it wol receive of this nature'. This was clarified in 1474–5 and the law then required that 26lb of brass be mixed with 1cwt of tin. Infringements of the law were treated severely. Bismuth was added in 1561 and in 1653 it was ordered that 3lb of bismuth (tin glass) should be mixed with every 1000lb of tin. Subsequently antimony was added to make an alloy of 100 parts tin, 8 parts antimony, 4 parts copper, and 4 parts bismuth.

Pewter items can not only be dated from their style, but also from the maker's mark known as the 'touch mark'. Reference to the appropriate textbooks will give guidance to dating (see page 48).

Britannia metal
A lead-free alloy of the pewter variety which consists of 5 per cent antimony, 3 per cent copper, and 92 per cent tin. It is frequently silver-plated but will, in its own right, polish up with a fine silvery lustre.

Identification of alloys
It is not possible with simple tests to identify all of the alloys of pewter, but it can be determined whether or not the object has a high lead content by rubbing one of its edges on a piece of white paper. The higher the lead content, the more the deposit of metal on the paper will resemble a pencil line. Conversely, the smaller the lead content, the fainter will be the line.

Brass
This is a yellow alloy of copper and zinc; the ingredients are used in varying proportions to produce alloys to suit particular applications. Common yellow brass is 50 per cent zinc and 50 per cent copper, is generally hard, and in the case of Delta metal, has almost the tensile strength of steel. Most of the alloys remain malleable and ductile, particularly Muntz metal which is 60 per cent copper and 40 per cent zinc.

Pinchbeck
A type of brass named after Christopher Pinchbeck (d. 1732), a London clockmaker who is said to have discovered it. It was extensively used in the last century to make inexpensive jewellery and watch cases, which are now collectors' items. The best pinchbeck consists of 89 per cent copper, 11 per cent zinc, to 93 per cent copper, 7 per cent zinc.

Gilding metal
An alloy of copper and zinc in the proportions of 80 to 20 is very suitable for the production of hollow-ware and jewellery which has to be plated. It is golden yellow in colour, ductile and malleable, but not as hard as common brass and has a melting point lower than copper.

Testing
A tiny drop of nitric acid applied to brass will cause a violent reaction giving a green froth. This is often useful for establishing whether a piece of jewellery is made of pinch-beck or gold, for the reaction on gold is negligible or, at most, very slow.

Fig 8   Testing with acid

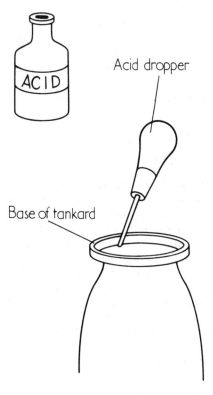

Acid dropper

Base of tankard

ACID

How far should renovation go?

The first thing to do is to assess the amount and type of damage to be tackled, how much of the damage is to be removed, and how much should be left as an acceptable sign of the age of the object. A piece should be restored to a condition where it has that pleasing quality peculiar to well-maintained, well-used metal. The odd blemish, a little oxide around the joint between a handle and the main body, or in an embossed area, are all things that give an old piece that muted appearance which develops with age. Dirt, crustations of old polish, oxides, sulphides and corrosion should be removed, not only to improve the appearance, but to prevent further attack on and deterioration of the metal's surface. Dents which are ugly and spoil the form of an object should be removed. Parts that are missing or badly broken should be replaced with new ones of the correct design. This is where the renovator turns researcher when he has to establish the shape of a missing part.

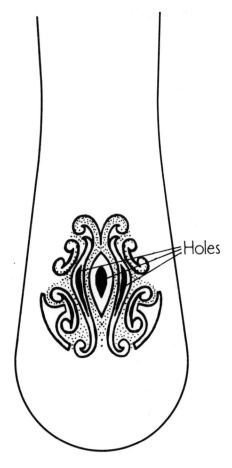

Fig 9   Wear on embossing

What cannot be repaired

Serious damage brought about by heavy use is generally irreversible, and damaged, heavily-worn objects should be left alone. When metal becomes worn and thin it is difficult to work, it invariably cracks, and may fall to pieces when manipulated. Examine objects carefully, in particular where there are raised parts such as an area of embossed design, where it is not uncommon to see the high spots worn off leaving tiny holes. A jeweller's magnifying glass of the

Fig 10   Jeweller's eyeglass

power 2X is useful for examining objects. If there is a dent, check to see if it has a smooth contour or if it has sharp creases with cracks which will open when a repair is attempted, for in such cases the metal is thin. Do not attempt to repair objects in such a condition. On knives or similar objects, examine the join between the handle and the blade

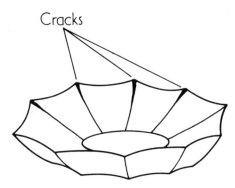

Cracks

Fig 11
Fluted brass dish displaying cracks down the fluting

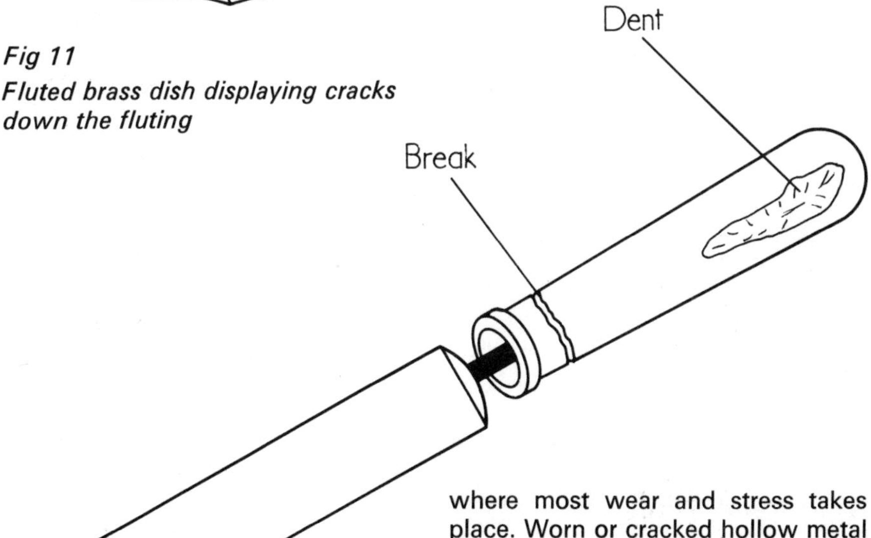

Dent

Break

Fig 11a
Repair of metal handles should be left to an expert

where most wear and stress takes place. Worn or cracked hollow metal handles are beyond the skill of the amateur renovator. A peculiarity of metals is age-hardening and brass is particularly susceptible to this. The condition is easily recognisable by obvious cracks which cannot be connected with any visible damage. When examined with a magnifying glass, a jagged crystalline feature may be seen in the crack. This condition is irreversible and renovation is impossible,

Removal of dents

When a dent occurs the metal is stretched, so in order to achieve a satisfactory repair further stretching of the metal must be avoided. Many would-be renovators pick up an old nailing hammer and merrily bash away. Not only do they transfer marks from the hammer face to the object, but they stretch the metal irrevocably. The object is usually beyond repair as a result of their efforts. This demonstrates the importance of two rules: (a) the force applied should be the minimum required and should only be applied for the minimum length of time. It should be well-thought out and applied in the correct place; (b) all tools should be impeccably clean and free from marks. Hammer faces should be polished and sharp edges rounded off.

First you must consider the type of metal from which the object is made, for that will influence the way in which the job should be tackled. A process of identification must be carried out (see metals identification, pp. 4–7). Having identified the metal, the following characteristics will help to indicate the problems which may arise.

Silver
Presents few problems as it is a fine, ductile, malleable metal, providing it has not worn too thin.

Silver plate
The base metal can be brass, copper, nickel, or nickel silver (see p. 5). Whichever it is, it may not be possible to remove the dent without damaging the plated surface. Use the

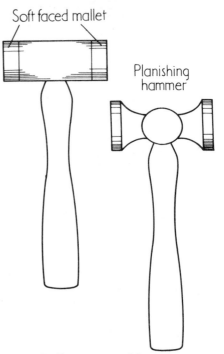

Soft faced mallet

Planishing hammer

Fig 12 Two types of hammer

minimum of force, and in the event of the plate being damaged, it will have to be repolished and replated. There are firms who specialize in this type of work (see pp. 46–47). It is advisable to send items for replating to them, because it is beyond the scope of the average repair workshop.

Silver plate on britannia metal
Britannia metal has often been used as a base metal for silver-plating. It is a soft, pewter-like alloy. If it is treated with care it will respond to gentle operations involving pressure and burnishing.

Brass
Brass should present few problems, but look out for cracks caused by age hardening.

10

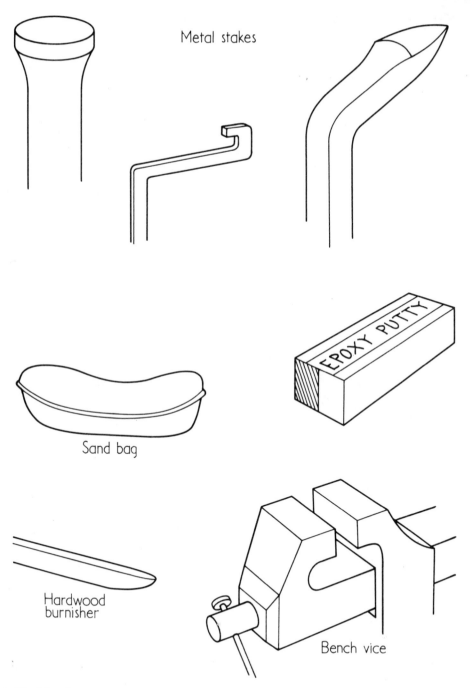

Metal stakes

Sand bag

EPOXY PUTTY

Hardwood
burnisher

Bench vice

Fig 13   Some useful equipment

11

Removal of dents

Principles of dent removal

One method is to support the dent against a surface which conforms as nearly as possible to the original form. Then apply a force which pushes the dent against that contoured surface. The tool with the contoured surface is known as a 'stake', and the force which pushes out the dent is applied either with hand pressure or with a soft-faced mallet.

Another method is to place the dented object on a soft surface such as a sandbag or folded blanket, and apply pressure with a contoured surface made either of steel or hardwood, using a moving action. This is known as 'burnishing' the dent. Never use a ball-ended hammer to remove a dent because the effect will be to stretch the metal and produce a series of small dents in the opposite direction to the original one, which will be difficult and in some cases impossible, to remove. Always make a careful appraisal of the problems likely to be encountered before starting to remove a dent, and never begrudge the time spent in making a stake or burnisher of the correct shape to tackle the job.

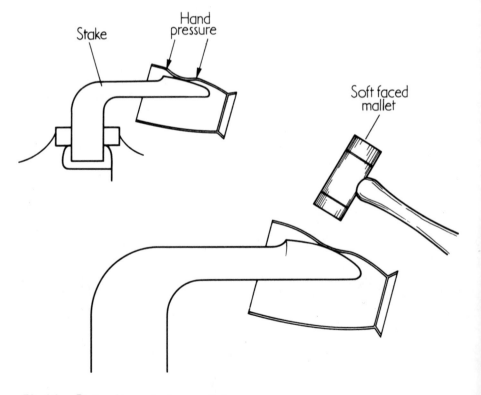

Fig 14   Removing a dent on a stake

Tools required
1 Nylon or hard rubber-faced mallet.
2 Flat-faced planishing hammer.
3 Stakes.
4 Epoxy resin putty.
5 Sand bag.
6 Hardwood for burnishers.
7 Strong bench and engineer's vice.

Preparation of tools
The soft-faced mallet requires no preparation except to clean the faces with a cloth if it is in good condition. Should the faces have foreign matter embedded in them or otherwise be uneven, they should be rubbed down with fine sandpaper, and then cleaned with a cloth. The flat-faced planishing hammer has to have its faces carefully prepared and polished. The edges of these faces must be rounded off because a sharp edge can cause a great deal of damage. Steel stakes must have their working surfaces clean and polished. Hardwood burnishers should be rubbed with progressively finer grades of glass paper until not only the contour is correct, but the surface is perfectly smooth.

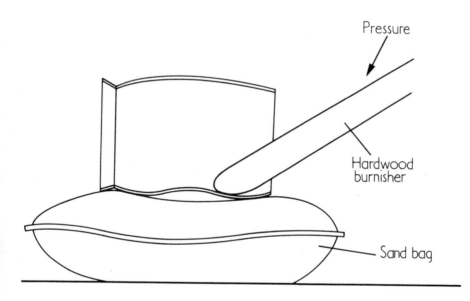

Fig 15 Removing a dent by burnishing

13

Removal of dents

Method

The object shown in Figure 16 illustrates a typical dent, in this case in the side of a teapot. A stake is selected which conforms to the internal shape of the teapot before it was dented. Steel stakes can be obtained from jewellers' suppliers but they are expensive, and one needs a whole range of shapes to cope with the variety of curvatures one is liable to encounter in renovation work. An alternative is to shape a piece of hardwood with rasps and glass paper. With the development of modern epoxy putty, a substance has come to the hand of the renovator which simplifies the work. It is purchased in a pack containing two different coloured putty-like substances which are coloured so as to assist even mixing. It is inexpensive and available from tool suppliers and some garages. Equal amounts of the substances are taken and kneaded together until a consistent colour is obtained. Plastic or rubber gloves must be worn. The putty is then pressed on to an undented surface of the teapot which has previously been smeared with grease to act as a release agent. A bolt of iron rod is then pressed into the putty which will be used as a handle later on. After the putty has solidified, it will be seen to have formed the exact contour of the undented part of the teapot, thus making an excellent stake.

The next step is to grip the stake in a vice and position the dent over it. Hand pressure may be enough to push out the dent; if not, a few well-placed blows with the nylon or rubber-faced mallet will do the trick. Creasing or stretch marks may then be removed by light planishing with the planishing hammer while the object is held against the stake.

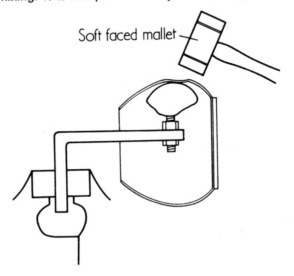

Soft faced mallet

Fig 16   Removing a dent from a teapot

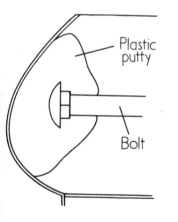

Plastic
putty

Bolt

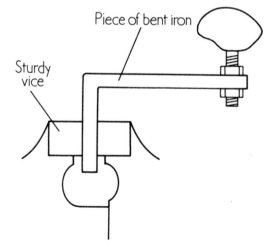

Piece of bent iron

Sturdy
vice

Fig 17   Making a plastic putty stake

Removal of dents

For dents in awkward places, like a narrow-necked vase where there is insufficient room to admit the normal stake, a tool called a 'snarling iron' can be made. This is a cranked length of steel rod; one end has a head which conforms to the contour of the internal shape of the object, the other end is held firmly in a vice. The dent in the vase is firmly held on to the contoured head of the tool. The shaft of the snarling iron is then struck with a hammer. Use an old household hammer because the steel may damage the surface of a good one. The shock from the hammer blow will be transmitted through the flexible shaft of the tool and push out the dent.

When a dent is in a hollow form, eg, a hollow bracelet, there are no means of working on one side of the dent. It is possible to silver solder a wire to the centre of the dent and pull it out. The dent may have to be pulled in more than one place to remove it, and then the solder has to be filed off. This method cannot be used on pewter, because soft solder is not strong enough to withstand the tension required to pull out a dent.

Planishing

When a dent has been removed by one of the methods previously described, it may be necessary to carry out further work to remove kinks or creases. This can be done with a planishing hammer prepared in the manner described. The job is placed on the stake and is struck very lightly with the planishing hammer to ensure

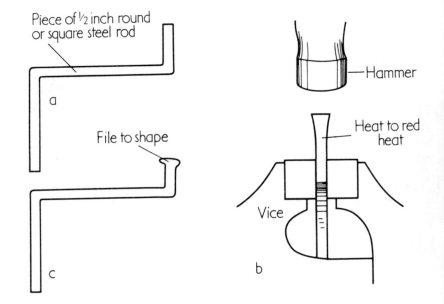

Fig 18   Making a snarling iron

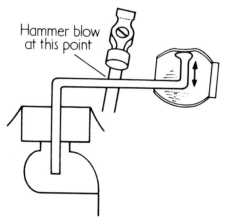

Hammer blow at this point

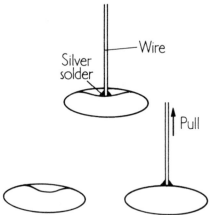

Wire

Silver solder

Pull

Fig 19   Removing a dent by using a snarling iron

Fig 20   Pulling out a dent

that it is supported on the stake at the correct point. A dull sound is emitted if the job is correctly supported on the stake, but if incorrectly supported a hollow ringing sound is produced. The sound is important because the object must be impinged between the planishing hammer and the stake, otherwise a dent will be created. Do not hammer heavily or the metal will be stretched, but tap sufficiently to achieve the desired effect and then cease. Planishing requires a great deal of skill, and should be used with discretion by the amateur for it is an operation that can cause serious damage if wrongly applied. It is well worth practising on some object of little value before working on a prized piece.

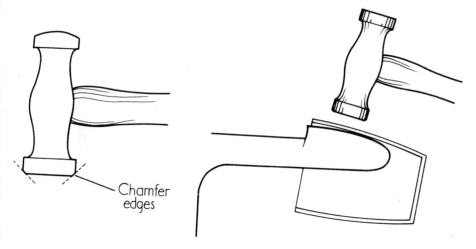

Chamfer edges

Fig 21   Planishing

Soldering

One of the best ways to join two pieces of metal is to apply a molten alloy to the join. When set the alloy makes a strong rigid bond. Briefly this explains the technique known as soldering.

There are two types of soldering, namely, hard and soft. In principle the difference is that the former is carried out at high temperatures (over 600°C) using solders which are often alloys containing silver, and the latter is burned out at low temperatures (300°C) using tin alloys as solder. In practice the two types are not compatible on the same object and one should adhere to the following rules.

1 Identify, through examination with a magnifying glass, which type of solder has been previously used on the object. Soft solder has a dull grey surface, whereas silver solder has a lustrous hard surface. A good repairer tries to conceal his work and previous repairs using soft solder may be difficult to perceive, especially if the object has been electro-plated after repair or assembly. Use the point of a penknife to scrape joints and then examine with the magnifying glass.

2 Never attempt to hard solder an object which has been previously soft soldered unless the latter is thoroughly cleaned from the surface, using the techniques described later.

3 Never soft solder silver objects.

4 Try to avoid the temptation to soft solder objects that have been assembled using hard solders.

5 Never attempt to hard solder pewter because the melting point of this alloy is very low and it is only possible to soft solder it.

6 In all soldering operations, cleanliness is of paramount importance. All solders, surfaces to be soldered, soldering hearths, irons and other equipment must be scrupulously clean.

7 Never soft solder on the same hearth as used for silver soldering.

8 Keep separate soldering areas, perferably at either end of the workshop, one for hard and one for soft soldering.

Hard soldering

What can be soldered by the amateur?
Certain hard soldering operations are within the scope of the amateur, but some are not. A successful renovator should know the limits of his skills and work within them. Silver is relatively easy to solder when one is dealing with small, simple repairs such as soldering a spoon handle. Large hollow-ware objects such as teapots or candlesticks are more difficult, and the problems are such that it is not feasible to attempt the work without some professional tuition. It is recommended that experience be gained on trial pieces of little value before attempting the real thing. Figure 22 shows the sort of work that is feasible.

Fig 22
Some examples of items that can be soldered

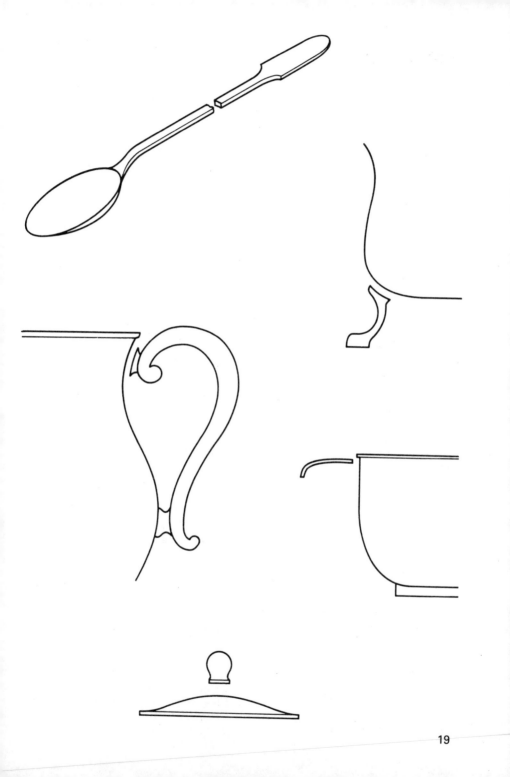

Soldering

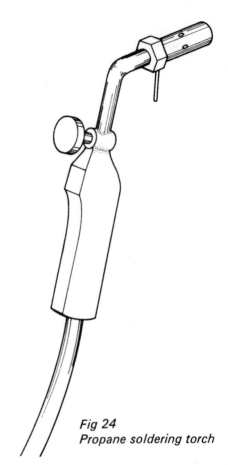

Equipment

1   A brazing torch will be required like the propane type shown in Figure 24. It is portable, easy to use, and has a wide range of flame sizes. For large objects something more powerful will be required, but there are many propane gas appliances on the market which are very suitable for the purpose.

2   A soldering hearth made in the manner illustrated and supported on a strong bench.

3   A pair of strong tweezers and a pointer made from a large darning needle pushed into a cork for a handle. The pointer is used to clear debris and adjust the position of the solder during soldering.

4   A small cheap paint brush for applying flux to the solder and the metals to be joined.

5   Heated crock, pyrex, or lead container to warm 10 per cent sulphuric acid solution (battery acid or one of the proprietary non-acid pickles).

Fig 24
Propane soldering torch

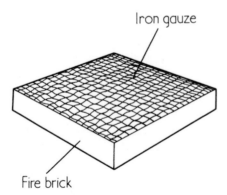

Iron gauze

Fire brick

Fig 23   A soldering hearth

WARNING   If concentrated acid has to be diluted to achieve the correct solution, always wear goggles and always add the acid to the water. NEVER add water to acid because it will react violently, and may cause serious injury.

Solders and fluxes

Soldering silver

It is important to use the correct hard solder for the metal concerned. For silver there are high grade soldering alloys which are available from

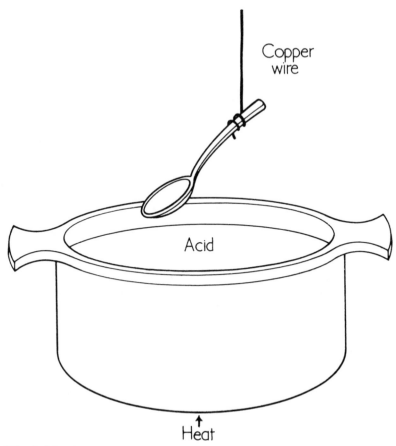

Copper wire

Acid

Heat

Fig 25 Acid pot

bullion dealers and other suppliers. These have several melting points commonly termed hard, medium and easy, but for repair work, medium and easy are the ones to use, as they have the lowest melting points.

The flux to use is called Borax, which is supplied in the form of a white cone. It is ground on the surface of a piece of slate with water to produce a milky solution. This is applied to the solder and to the area being soldered with a paint brush. Borax cones and slates are available from jewellers' suppliers.

Hard solders for brass and bronze

These are often called silver solders but in fact they have a very low silver content, if any, and should not be used on silver. There is a whole range of these solders, alloyed to suit the metals referred to. It is, therefore, necessary to ask suppliers for a solder suitable for the metal concerned. Special fluxes are supplied with these solders which are available from welding and brazing suppliers. The soldering procedure is exactly the same as that described for silver.

Soldering

Removing soft solder

Should the piece being renovated be contaminated with soft solder, it is essential to remove the solder before hard soldering is carried out. The procedure is to gently heat the object over a flame. Do not overheat or the soft solder will eat in and spoil the job. As soon as the solder melts, brush it off with a stiff bristle brush. This procedure may have to be carried out two or three times to remove the greater part of the soft solder. There should then be a thin film of solder remaining which can be dissolved by immersing the object for about half an hour in slightly diluted hydrochloric acid. It may require more than one immersion before the desired result is achieved, The surface is then cleaned to a bright finish with a file or emery paper, and examined for contamination with a magnifying glass.

Protecting other solder joints

Invariably the object being repaired will have many solder joints which were made when it was first constructed, and these will have to be protected from the effects of an additional soldering operation. Establish where the original ones are and paint them with a thick mixture of jeweller's rouge powder and water. This mixture should be applied carefully with a fine brush and should not be allowed to contaminate the new solder joint or the solder or flux being used. Select a solder with a low melting point (easy) for objects with more than one solder joint.

Soldering procedure

Figure 27 illustrates a spoon with a broken handle which will be used as an example.

1   Ensure that the two faces to be joined are clean by filing them square.
2   Set up the spoon so that it is well supported using pieces of steel which have been blued in a flame.
3   Select a solder alloy with a suitable melting point. In this instance, providing care is taken, the assembly join between bowl and stem is unlikely to be disturbed, so a medium melting point solder is used because it has a better colour. 'Easy' solders tend to be yellow in colour but are necessary when soldering close to an existing joint which may be disturbed by reheating.
4   Cut the solder into suitable sized pieces.
5   Paint the join with flux, together with the piece of solder, which is then placed on the join.
6   Heat the area gently at first so that the moisture in the flux evaporates slowly and does not boil, so displacing the solder.
7   The full heat of the flame can now be applied and the pointer used to

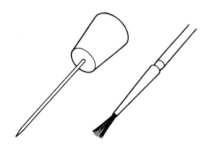

Fig 25a
A needle pointer and paint brush
for flux

adjust the position of the solder which should contact the metal on each side of the join. Ensure that the two pieces being joined receive the same amount of heat because solder runs to the hottest point. The correct condition can only be achieved by closely watching the colour of the metal when it is being heated. Solders flow at just red heat, so that if each part reaches the correct temperature simultaneously, the solder will flow neatly into the space by capillary action.

8 Inspect the joint with a magnifying glass to ensure that the solder has flushed through to the other side. If it has not then apply more flux, and possibly more solder if the join looks short of it, and reheat. When cool, the spoon is placed in the hot acid (or non-acid pickle). This will remove the flux oxides from the surface of the metal. Never leave an object in the solution for more than a few minutes because both solder and metal may be attacked. The procedure is the same for brass and copper. After soldering silver, there is often the problem of 'fire stain'. This is dealt with under 'Refinishing', p. 44.

Fig 26   *Cutting solder*

Fig 27   Repairing a spoon handle

Soldering

Soft soldering

Do not carry out soft soldering operations in the same area as that used for hard soldering. Have a separate hearth to minimize the risk of contaminating the hard soldering area.

Equipment for soft soldering

1 A soldering torch for heating soldering irons, and a gentle heating flame such as is produced by the lighting jet of a gas cooker, which has a flexible lead and gives a soft, pencil flame. Never use hard, hot flames for soft soldering. Propane torches, specially designed for the purpose, can be obtained from jewellers' suppliers.

2 A soldering hearth constructed in the manner described in Figure 23, p. 20.

3 An electric or gas heated soldering iron.

4 A pointer made from a large darning needle pushed into a cork to form a handle (see Fig 25a, p. 22). This is used to position solder and to clear debris during soldering.

5 A wooden stick like a cocktail stick for applying flux before and during soldering. Sometimes it is helpful to smear a little flux over solder to get it to flow smoothly.

Solders and fluxes

Most soft solders are alloys of tin and are available in stick form or as wire, often with the flux as a core. The most common is that used by plumbers which requires separate flux paste. Cored solders are very good for localized joins such as electrical connections or for small components. For

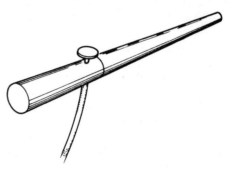

Fig 28
Soft soldering torch

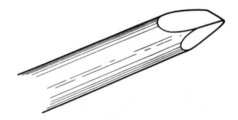

Fig 29
Soldering iron

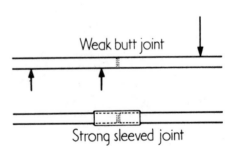

Fig 30
Strong and weak solder joints

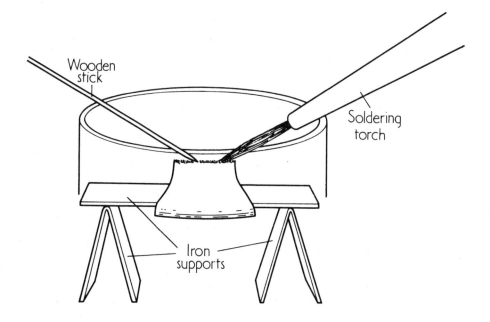

Fig 31   Soldering on a handle

large areas of solder, the separate flux is preferable because it can be spread to give a perfect covering of the area. Advice can be sought from DIY stores regarding the various soft solders which are available. Brass, copper and pewter (see 'Soldering pewter', p. 28) may all be joined with soft solder, but never use it on silver because it will debase the metal and devalue the piece.

Where to use soft solder

Because soft solder will not tolerate much heat, stress or strain, the type of repairs for which it is used must be carefully considered. Figure 30 illustrates weak and strong joints. Techniques of riveting, dovetailing, or applying a patch may have to be used to achieve a joint of the required strength. Figure 30 shows that soft solder is at its weakest point when in a state of 'peel' and would be unsuitable for repairing the spoon handle which has been successfully repaired with hard solder. Figure 30 shows a sleeved joint which makes an obviously strong repair in conjunction with soft solder.

As previously mentioned, brass and copper may easily be soft soldered, and after a little practice both large and small objects may be soldered by the amateur. Pewter may also be soft soldered but it is particularly difficult to do so because it has a melting point which is close to that of soft solder. Pewter is treated later as a special case. As in the case of hard soldering. practise on scrap metal or on objects that have little value before attempting to work on the piece being renovated.

Soldering

The soldering iron

There are two types of soldering iron: (a) the simple copper ended one which is heated in a flame, and (b) the electric type. Both are available in a variety of sizes and a good weighty one should be selected for repair work. As they get dirty with use they must be cleaned with an old file or emery paper and then 'tinned' with solder. This is done in the following way for the non-electric type. Heat the copper bit of the iron in the flame, rotating it slowly. When it has reached the correct temperature a moving pattern of colours will be seen on the copper. Do not get the bit red-hot. At this point it should be dipped in flux and quickly coated with solder. The iron is then ready for use. The electric iron should be treated in the same way but it is not heated over a flame. Such irons have pre-set temperature regulators.

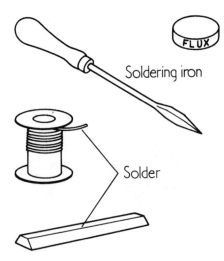

Soldering iron

Solder

Fig 32   Some equipment for soft soldering

26

Soft soldering procedure

A typical soft soldering joint is shown in Figure 33, in this case a bracket from an old bulb horn.

1   Clean the surfaces to be joined using emery paper and files to remove old solder and to obtain bright clean surfaces.

2   Offer up the two components to each other to ensure that they fit together accurately.

3   Smear both surfaces with flux.

4   Cut off a piece of solder and place it on one of the soldering faces, in this case that of the bracket. Then heat the component until the solder melts. It should be evenly spread over the surface using the 'tinned' soldering iron. The other face is then 'tinned' with solder using the soldering iron.

5   Clean and flux the tinned surface and bring the two parts together. They can be bound in position with iron binding wire (0·5mm diameter). Once in position, gently heat both components with the gas lighting jet until the solder melts. The wooden stick smeared with flux can be run round the edge of the soldering to clean it and improve its finish. Do not overheat and do not move the components until the solder has solidified.

6   Flux and dirt may be washed off with hot water, and the oxides polished off using one of the finishing techniques described under 'Cleaning and polishing', pp. 42–45.

Small components and thin metal may be joined to other parts by fluxing, then tinning with the soldering iron loaded with solder. Place in position and heat by conduction, by applying the hot soldering iron firmly to them. This is commonly called a 'sweated joint'.

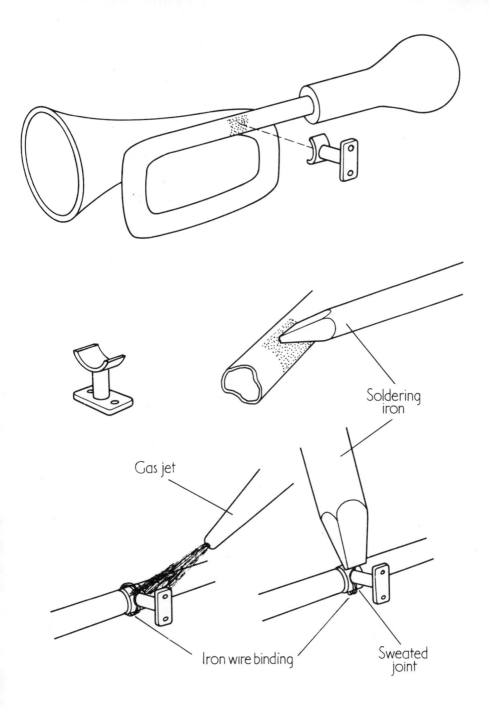

Soldering
iron

Gas jet

Iron wire binding

Sweated
joint

Fig 33 Soldering a bracket to a brass horn

Soldering

Soldering pewter

Small soldering repairs can be carried out using the soldering iron and soft solder, or preferably a specially formulated solder and flux as follows.

Solder

Proportions by weight, 2 parts tin, 2 parts lead, 1 part bismuth. Melt these together and pour the melt into grooves in a piece of wood to produce handy strips. Alternatively, pieces of old pewter or britannia metal may be used for solder.

Flux

Proportions by volume, 5 parts glycerine, 12 parts distilled water, 5 parts zinc chloride. The latter can be made by putting zinc into hydrochloric acid until the bubbling stops. Alternatively, one of the soft soldering paste fluxes may be used.

Figure 34 depicts a pewter tankard whose handle has pulled off taking with it a piece out of the main body. This will be used as an example.

1 Clean the area to be soldered with detergent, hot water, and a stiff brush (a toothbrush is ideal). Then scrape the edges of the joint with the point of a sharp knife to remove oxides.

2 Push the handle back into position and bind it with iron binding wire.

3 Flux the area.

4 Load the previously tinned soldering iron with solder.

5 Apply it to the join and hold it there until the pewter has been heated sufficiently to fuse with the solder.

6 Apply solder to the point of the iron as necessary and gradually work round until the joint is complete.

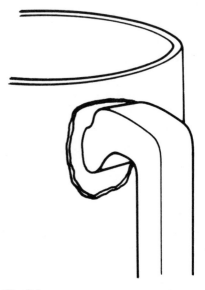

Fig 34
Scrape edge of break until clean and bright

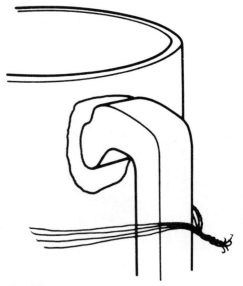

Fig 35
Bind handle in position with iron wire

28

Great care should be taken; it is easy to melt the pewter and make a hole in it. Unless you are very experienced, do not touch pewter with a flame.

If you wish to try soldering with a flame use a soft flame. The lighting jet of a gas cooker is good for pewter, if, as previously stated, the renovator is very experienced.

Method

Clean the join to be soldered, flux it, position the solder, and heat with the flame until the solder runs. Use a gentle flame to heat up the whole area, but take care not to overheat. A hard flame should be avoided. The application of the soldering iron at this stage may give a little localized heat to assist the solder to run.

Eruptions, holes and cracks in pewter

This type of damage is common in pewter. Eruptions and holes require radical treatment. They should be cleaned by drilling out until bright fresh metal is exposed. This is then plugged with pewter, fluxed and soldered in the manner described. Cracks should be cleaned by cutting through them with a fret-saw blade (see p. 32) to expose bright metal. A piece of pewter should then be fashioned to fit and soldered in place. If the surface is uneven this can be rectified by carving it with a sharp knife because pewter is soft. Finishing can then be done as described under 'Refinishing', p. 44.

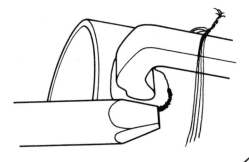

Fig 36
Flux joint and melt pewter solder with tinned soldering iron

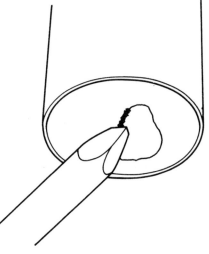

Fig 37
Treat the inside in the same way

Making handles and knobs

Handles and knobs, such as those on teapots, are very often made in ebony, rosewood or ebonite. The latter is a black compressed composition of paper. A good handyman can make new ones. The following simple tools are required :
1   Stout bench.
2   Sawing peg and clamp for clamping objects to the bench.
3   Coping or fret-saw and suitable blades.
4   Thin brass for templates.
5   Suitable materials – ebony, rosewood or ebonite.
6   Piece of softwood for model.
7   Craft knife and chisels.

If the handle or knob is simply broken, it may be possible to repair it by the following method. You not only glue it using a good waterproof glue, but also drill and pin it. Ensure that the pieces are clamped together in the appropriate position, and then drill as shown, ensuring that the drill penetrates deep into the other part of the handle or knob. The pin should be a tight fit in the hole and must be pushed in with plenty of glue. If possible the ends of the pins should be peened over.

If the handle is beyond repair, then a new one will have to be made. Select a piece of wood of the appropriate type and thickness. If a fibre handle is required, use a piece of ebonite. If enough of the old handle

Fig 38
Repairing a wooden or fibre handle

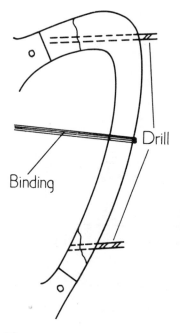

Fig 39
Bind the broken edges together and drill as shown

30

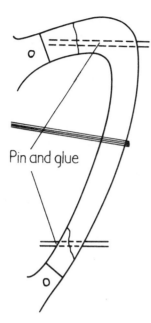

Pin and glue

Fig 40   Pin and glue

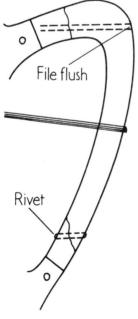

File flush

Rivet

Fig 41
File the pins flush with the handle

remains, a pencil can be run round it transferring the outline on to new material, which can then be cut out using the fret-saw (see Sawpiercing p. 32).

If there is insufficient of the old handle to copy, then choose a suitable pattern for the new handle. Valuable information can be obtained from reference books from which you can make a drawing and then a model. The thin brass sheet can be cut out to the outline with the fret-saw. Try this profile in position on the object being repaired and check how it will fit and look. Use a pencil to mark round the brass profile on to a piece of soft wood and cut it out with the fret-saw. The model handle is then fettled and carved until it looks and feels right. A new handle can be made in the appropriate material, using the model as a pattern, and can then be fitted to the object (see riveting, p. 36).

Knobs are made in much the same way as handles. It is possible to buy ebony, rosewood and ebonite in round sections, which can be drilled, filed and carved into shape. Knobs which are made in metal can be cast, using the methods described for casting on p. 38.

Finishing the wood or ebonite
The handle or knob must be carefully rubbed down with successively finer grades of glass paper until a very smooth surface is achieved. No further finishing process is required with these woods, but they may be rubbed with teak oil or wax. Ebonite should be treated in the same way with successively finer grades of glass paper and finally polished with chrome cleaning polish as described on p. 42.

Sawpiercing and replacing inlay

The renovator will find that a fret-saw is a very useful tool for a number of jobs which involve cutting out wood or metal. There are several sizes from which suitable saws should be selected. It is desirable to have two saws, a shallow one for small work, and a deep one for large work. It is important to select a blade which is suitable to cut the material being handled. Thinner finer-toothed blades are required for metal than for wood. The following chart of blade thicknesses may assist in deciding the appropriate blade to be used.

Thick blades
Numbers 4 and 3, suitable for wood.
Number 2, suitable for wood or metal.

Thin blades
Number 1, suitable for wood or metal.
Numbers 0, 2/0 and 3/0, suitable for thin wood or metal.

Equipment required
1 A rigid support for the object being worked on.
2 Fret-saw and suitable blades.
3 Gambouge powder and methylated spirits, or white water-colour paint.
4 Scriber.
5 Tracing paper.
6 Pencils.

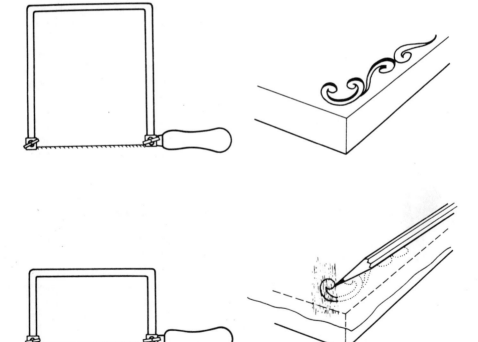

Fig 42   Fret-saw frames

Fig 43   Replacing brass inlay

Figure 43 shows a piece of brass inlay which is missing from the lid of a rosewood box, and will be used to illustrate the sawpiercing technique. It applies equally to both wood and metal.

Establish the required material thickness first by carefully lifting some of the existing inlay and measuring it with a micrometer. If there is no means of ascertaining the thickness of the inlay, then take a sample to the metal supplier who will be able to advise.

Having obtained the correct material for the inlay, clean out the recess, remove old glue by scraping with a craft knife, and then make an accurate tracing of the shape of the inlay. Lay tracing paper over the shape to be filled and rub over it with a soft pencil until the outline appears, as in Figure 43. Remove the paper and turn it over so that the reverse side is uppermost. Then place it on a piece of white paper so that the outline is more easily visible. Using the soft pencil go round the outline so that it is distinct on the reverse side. Gambouge powder (which can be obtained from tool suppliers) mixed with methylated spirits is then used to coat the surface of the metal. Alternatively, a thick coat of artist's white water-colour paint can be used for this purpose. After the coating has dried, place the tracing paper over the metal and rub over the paper with a hard pencil. This will transfer the pencil line from the back of the tracing paper on to the coating on the metal.

It is then necessary to scribe through the pencil line on the coated metal with a steel scriber which may be obtained from a tool supplier. Alternatively, a scriber may be made from a piece of tool steel or silver steel. Make sure the tool scratches into the metal. The coating can then be washed off leaving a fine accurate line which can easily be followed by the fret-saw.

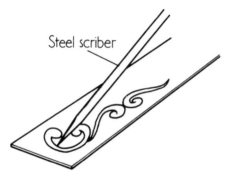

Steel scriber

Fig 44   Using a steel scriber

Sawpiercing and replacing inlay

Compress saw frame when fitting blade

Preparing the fret-saw and supporting the work piece

Select a blade of suitable thickness for the material being cut, in this case number 1. Unfasten the clamping screws on the saw frame, and after ensuring that the teeth of the blade are facing backwards, fasten the blade firmly into the front clamp. Press the front of the saw frame against the work-bench so as to compress it slightly and clamp the saw blade in the rearmost clamp. On releasing the pressure, the saw blade should be rigid under the tension of the saw frame. A fret-sawing support can either be made in wood or purchased from a tool supplier. The support should be firmly attached to the work-bench with a clamp. Position the workpiece over the 'V' in the support and start to saw. Keep the saw blade moving vertically, and lubricate the blade from time to time with beeswax or spittle. The blade should be kept to the outside of the scribed line, never down the middle or the inside, otherwise the metal cut out will be too small.

The new inlay is then offered up to the space in the box lid. It may have to be adjusted by filing to get it to fit accurately. Once this has been achieved, roughen the underside of the metal with coarse emery paper and coat it with epoxy glue, afterwards placing it in position. Place a polythene sheet over it, then a flat piece of wood, and clamp in position. The polythene prevents the excess glue adhering to the piece of wood used as the clamp support.

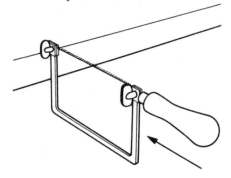
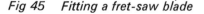

Compress saw frame when fitting blade

Fig 45 Fitting a fret-saw blade

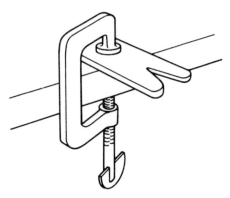

Fig 46 Fret-saw support

Finally, fasten a piece of emery paper to a block of wood and use it to carefully rub the piece of new inlay down to the same level as the surrounding wood. Finish this procedure by polishing with fine emery paper. Then clean the surface with methylated spirits and coat with a suitable lacquer.

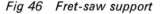

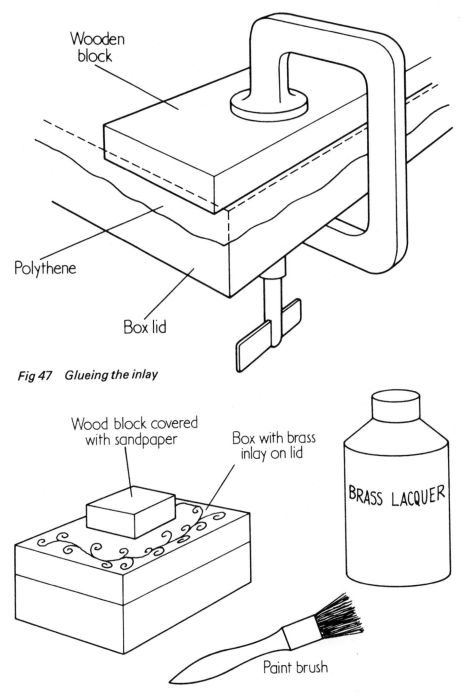

Wooden block

Polythene

Box lid

Fig 47   Glueing the inlay

Wood block covered
with sandpaper

Box with brass
inlay on lid

BRASS LACQUER

Paint brush

Fig 48   Rub down the inlay prior to lacquering

Pinning, riveting and cheniering

Handles, hinges, legs, and even the main body of an object, are frequently riveted. The rivet may become loose or break and needs to be replaced. It also may be necessary to use rivets in addition to solder to strengthen an otherwise weak joint.

There are two types of rivet: dome headed and countersunk flat headed. Whichever type is used the rivet must fit the hole accurately through which it passes. After removing the old rivet, the first job is to true the hole which may have become oval or enlarged. To do this, use either a twist drill which is a fraction larger than the existing hole, or a jeweller's broach, available in a range of sizes from jewellers' suppliers. The rivet can be made from wire which accurately fits the hole. Figure 50 shows the tools for making the rivet heads and those that can be made for the riveting operation.

Hinge pins and the pins that pass through handle sockets to hold wooden or ebonite handles in place, simply have their ends peened over. Hinge pins are best made in nickel silver wire for it is durable and will take the wear of continual opening and closing. Use a wire that is an accurate fit in the hinge, push it through, trim off with a pair of wire cutters and leave just enough wire protruding to peen over. This peening expands the end of the wire which can be filed off flush with the hinge. Pins for holding handles in place should be made of the same metal as the body of the object. Like the hinge pin, the wire should be a tight fit in the hole and peened in exactly

the same way. It may be necessary to run a drill or broach through the holes because the hole in the handle very often wears larger than the one in the metal socket. If this is the case, the handle will be unstable, so it is important to ensure that the pin should be a tight fit in the wood.

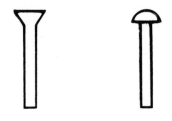

Fig 49   Types of rivet

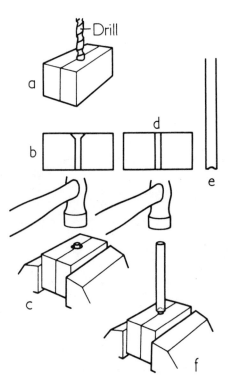

Cheniering

This technique is sometimes used by manufacturers to secure components of an object where parts are fragile, such as enamel decoration, and are not likely to withstand the pressures and percussive forces which have to be employed in riveting. A tube of similar metal to the object is attached to one component and then passed through a hole in the other component. The free end of the tube is then expanded with a special tool. Occasionally the tube becomes loose through wear, and this can be rectified by the method described. It should be emphasised that this technique is not one which the novice should use when riveting is possible.

Fig 51   A broach reamer and pin vice

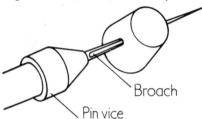

Broach

Pin vice

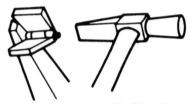

Fig 52   Riveting

Fig 50   (left) Making a rivet: a. Clamp two pieces of steel in a vice and drill between them, using a drill slightly smaller than the rivet wire; b. For a countersunk head, file the end of the hole to a funnel shape in each piece of steel; c. Clamp rivet wire between pieces of steel. Hammer protruding end which expands to fill funnel shape; d. For dome-headed rivets, do not file into funnel shape; e. Take a round steel rod, slightly larger than the rivet head, and drill an indentation in one end; f. Clamp rivet wire between the pieces of steel. Place indented end of steel rod on protruding end of wire and tap with hammer. The wire will take the form of the indent to produce a domed head

Fig 53   (right) Cheniering: a. Steel rod; b. File two tapering flats; c. File end to shape; centre pip should be wider at its thickest point than bore of tube; d. Place cheniering tool in drill, place pip in bore of tube and rotate using light pressure.

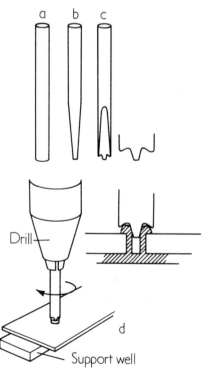

Casting new parts

Very often an object is minus a leg, knob or finial. It is possible for even a novice to cast a new part using simple methods. Pewter has a low melting point (320°C). It can be melted in a simple metal container, and then poured into plaster of Paris or papier mâché moulds. Silver and brass melt at a higher temperature (900–960°C) and must be melted in a fireclay crucible. Both metals may be poured into moulds made from cuttlefish bone, obtainable from pet shops which supply it for budgerigars.

Tools and equipment
1   Suitable melting pot made of iron for melting pewter. Flat fireclay crucible for melting silver and brass with simple sheet metal holder.
2   Pair of iron tongs.
3   Gas ring for melting the pewter. Powerful propane gas torch for silver and brass.
4   Large pieces of cuttlefish bone for casting brass and silver. Plaster of Paris or papier mâché for casting pewter.
5   Boric acid crystals or Borax as flux for brass and silver.
6   Materials for making patterns, that is, wood, pieces of wire, and epoxy putty or polyester resin filler.
7   Old pieces of silver, brass or pewter for melting down.

Making the casting pattern
It is important to identify the age and style of the object, and base the shape and form of the new part on an appropriate design. This will require research in reference books dealing with the historical aspect of design.

38

Having established what the replacement part should look like, a model should be made in wood, epoxy putty or filler. Make the model a little thicker than the part required, to allow for shrinkage during casting, and also to leave extra metal for fettling when casting is complete.

Figure 55 shows the technique for making a mould to cast pewter. Use a pewter alloy which matches the object being repaired. Modern hard lead-free pewter is bright in colour, so it is unsuitable for casting parts for old pewter. It is worth collecting a few old pewter objects which have no value or which are beyond repair as a source of metal for such castings. Melt the pewter in an iron pot on a gas ring and take care not to overheat. It may be easier to use an iron ladle to take the molten metal from the pot and pour it into the mould.

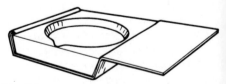

Fig 54

Melting pot for pewter and crucible for silver and brass

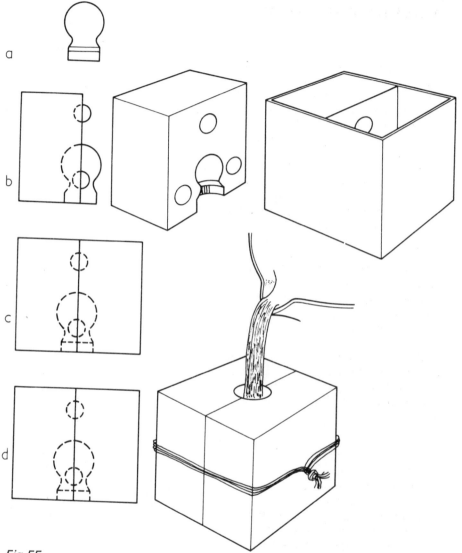

Fig 55

Casting pewter: a. Make a model of
the knob, from wood or epoxy resin
putty; b. Press the model and three
ball bearings halfway into plasticine.
Smear exposed half with grease;
c. Make a cardboard frame for the
mould; fill the other side with
plaster of Paris; d. Remove the
plasticine half, leaving the model
embedded in the plaster, and grease
exposed plaster face. Pour plaster
in to replace plasticine. Split the
mould, remove the model, bind the
two halves with iron wire. The
molten pewter is poured into the
mould and allowed to solidify

Casting new parts

Figure 56 shows the method for making the mould to cast brass and silver. These metals should be melted in a shallow fireclay crucible which can be obtained from a jewellers' supplier. Use a powerful propane gas flame to melt the metal; a small piece of borax or a pinch of boric acid crystals applied at red-hot heat will help to clear oxides. A black iron rod may be used to scrape away oxides prior to pouring the metal into the mould. Pouring should be speedy but smooth. The metal should enter and fill the mould in a continuous stream. If there is a break in pouring this may cause a fault line in the casting. It should be remembered that because of the high melting point of brass and silver, they solidify more quickly than pewter.

Brass and silver castings should be cleaned in hot acid pickle. Fettling should then be done with files and emery paper as described in 'Refinishing', p. 44.

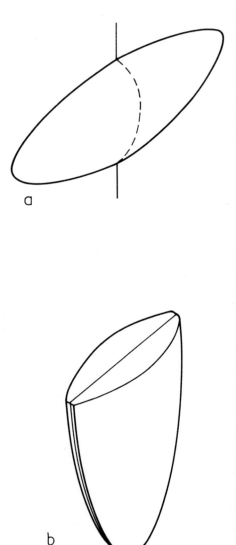

Fig 56
Casting silver and brass: a. Cut a large piece of cuttle bone in half; b. Smooth the two soft faces flat using emery paper; c. Press the model of the knob into one half; d. Cut a funnel for the molten metal and scratch two air holes with the point of a nail; e. Press other half of cuttle bone on to first half; push two skewers through both pieces so they can easily be found; f. Remove model, bind both pieces of cuttle together with wire then pour in molten silver or brass

Fig 56

40

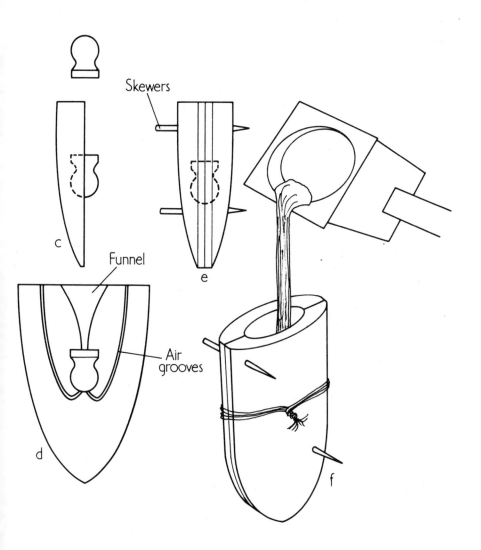

Skewers

Funnel

Air
grooves

c

d

e

f

Cleaning and polishing

This is a very important operation in the renovation cycle. For the three metals in question, methods should usually be gentle, and strong chemicals and coarse abrasives should be avoided. However, in certain circumstances radical methods have to be applied, such as in the case of heavy corrosion. The way to treat each of the metals will be dealt with first, followed by the methods of stripping the surface and repolishing which are necessary following a soldering operation or when corrosion is very severe.

In all cases, the first thing to do is to wash off all dirt and old polish deposits with warm water and detergent, applied with a bristle brush.

Silver

This should be treated as gently as possible because it is a soft metal which can easily be rubbed away. Special care should be taken where there is an embossed or raised pattern so as not to rub off the high spots. If there is a black sulphide layer present (often incorrectly called the oxide) this can be removed from the surface by using one of the dipping solutions which are available. If the object is too large to dip, place it in a plastic bowl and, wearing plastic gloves, douse the surface with the solution applied with cotton wool. This should be continued until the surface of the metal is white. Then polish with silver polish on a soft cloth to create a bright finish. On intricate surfaces such as engraving or embossing, use a fairly stiff bristle brush with silver polish, or alternatively, a paste composed of either jewellers' rouge and water, or whitening (chalk) and water. Once a good polish has been achieved it is important to carry out regular light cleaning so reducing the amount of wear. After treatment with the dipping solution, persistent corrosion can be rubbed with a fine brass wire brush (known as a scratch brush) used with copious quantities of a solution of warm water, liquid detergent and a splash of ammonia. If the corrosion still persists, it can be treated with a fibre-glass brush (known as a glass brush) which can be obtained from jewellers' suppliers. This brush is very abrasive so it must be used with great care. If the surfaces are so badly attacked that they do not respond to any of these treatments, then refinishing may be necessary.

Silver plate

This should be treated in the same way as silver, but even more care is necessary because of the additional risk of rubbing through the plated surface and exposing the base metal. Beware of prolonged rubbing on raised surfaces, edges and corners. On embossed surfaces use the same brushing techniques as described for silver.

Pewter

With age, pewter develops a patina (oxide) which, if the object has been regularly cleaned and polished, develops into a pleasant, muted, mature surface with a dull shine. However, if the patina has been allowed to develop unchecked, it becomes a thick brittle layer with an unpleasant black colour. It is possible to remove the patina by immersing the object in a caustic soda solution, or in a solution of hydrochloric acid. This is a radical step because the removal of the thick oxide will often leave a pitted surface, and worse still, trigger off a reaction which causes small bubbles of pewter to quake up months after the chemical treatment. The reason for this is that old pewter (100–300 years) has oxidised, not only on the surface, but into the grain structure of the metal alloy. Some of the metals in the alloy are more prone to this attack than others. Together, the metal and oxide have a consistent appearance; dissolve the oxide and one is left with pits, cracks and fissures which the metal oxides have vacated. Worse still, this chemical attack on the oxide permeates the grain structure of the metal and continues reacting with the oxide remaining, so causing the eruptions described. Chemicals are, therefore, to be used with the utmost care, and should not be used on very old and valuable pieces, especially if they have intricate marks or engraving. Just polish with furniture polish and leave well alone.

If the pewter is reasonably clean then regular cleaning with a good metal polish will maintain and improve the appearance. This may be preserved to some extent by spraying the object with one of the silicone spraying fluids used to insulate car ignition systems from moisture.

If there is an ugly scale present, remove it gradually, working on a small area at a time using the following methods. Apply a solution of household cleaning detergent powder to a section, scatter a little of the detergent powder on the dampened area and rub with a pumice block or coarse wet-or-dry paper. This should be carried on until areas of bright metal are revealed. Change to a medium grit wet-or-dry paper (400–600) and work it with the detergent solution as a lubricant. To keep the surface contour even, change the direction of the rubbing frequently. Do not use wire wool. Continue until the finest wet-or-dry paper has been used, and then work across the object with metal polish applied with a piece of leather stretched and fastened to a piece of wood (see Figure 57). A lot of hard rubbing will be necessary before the required finish is obtained.

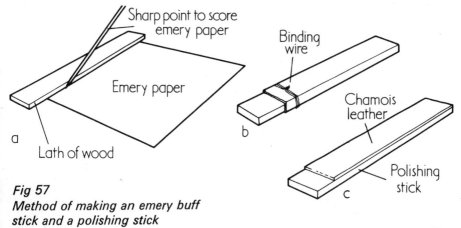

Fig 57
Method of making an emery buff stick and a polishing stick

Cleaning and polishing

Brass
If brass has been kept in a damp atmosphere without regular cleaning, it will probably have a thick, greenish-black deposit on the surface. This is very difficult to remove by simple rubbing techniques. It is much easier to start by using the following methods. Make up a strong solution of washing-up liquid, warm water and ammonia. Allow the object to soak for some time, giving it an occasional rub with a fine brass wire brush. When this treatment is complete, a dull brass-coloured surface should appear. Normal polishing will usually prove effective, using the method outlined for silver with appropriate brass polishes. Some chrome cleaning pastes sold in tubes are also very effective. Certain brands have white aluminium oxide as a constituent which has excellent polishing qualities. Once the object is clean, regular light cleaning is preferable to infrequent heavy applications of the polishing abrasive.

Refinishing
When the surface of a metal requires resurfacing, either as a result of corrosion, scratching, dents or removal of excess solder following a soldering operation, the procedure outlined in this section should be followed.

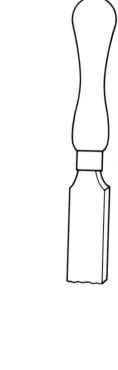

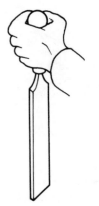

Fig 58   Fitting a file handle

Tools required

1 A 1 × 8in smooth cut flat file and handle; two $\frac{1}{2}$ × 6in half round files with handles, one smooth cut, the other medium.

2 Four laths of wood 1 × 12 × $\frac{1}{4}$in; twelve inches of $\frac{3}{8}$in diameter dowel; sheets of emery paper grades 1, 0, 00; wet-or-dry paper, 400, 600 and 800.

3 A piece of 'Water of Ayre' stone.

4 Soft leather (chamois) polishing cloths, and the polishing medium which suits the metal being treated.

Preparation of tools

New files should be treated in the following way. Dip them in turpentine and holding the tip downwards, light the turpentine. Allow it to burn freely along the whole length of the file until all of the turpentine has burned away. This tempers the file, making it less brittle and more suitable for soft metals. The handle must then be fitted. The best method of doing this is to heat the tang to a red heat and push the handle on to it. Final tightening is achieved by holding the handle firmly in one hand, and hitting it with a hammer or mallet. Do not allow the file to rest against any hard surface while doing so or it may break. Finally rub chalk thoroughly into the teeth of the file to prevent them becoming clogged with metal.

Buffing and polishing sticks should be prepared as shown in Figure 57.

Removing scratches, marks, unwanted engraving and excess solder

An object may be scratched, have superfluous engraved inscriptions, or have excess solder on the surface following a soldering operation. These blemishes have to be removed by filing the metal away. In the case of pewter which is very soft, a scraping tool such as a craft knife may be used.

First you must support the object against a firm surface such as a bench top. Never try to file an unsupported object because it will be impossible to do so accurately. Use as large a file as is reasonably possible. Small files are only suitable for small intricate areas. A large file will spread its effect over a larger area and give a more even surface. All traces of the blemish must be removed before the next stage. In the case of an engraved inscription, watch the lettering carefully during the filing operation. The deep parts of the inscription will be the last to go, and if they disappear in unison, this will indicate that an even amount of metal has been removed.

Having removed the blemish, the next stage is to remove the file marks with the emery buff stick. Start with the coarsest grade and work across the direction of the file marks until they have been eradicated. Then using the medium emery, work across the direction of the previous operation and so on, working across the direction of the previous stage until a fine, slightly matt finish is obtained. The metal is then ready to polish.

Fire stain

Fire stain affects silver when it has been heated to a dull red heat. Its appearance is slightly greyer than the unaffected silver, often in patches. One solution is to grind the surface with the 'Water of Ayre' stone and water, or with buff sticks, thus removing the surface layer containing the fire stain. This is followed by polishing. Or, heat the object once or twice to induce an even fire stain over the entire surface. Clean the object in acid pickle (see p. 40) and repolish.

Useful addresses

Mountford Rubber Co.
101 Bracebridge Street,
Birmingham 6.

Ebonite, rubber, fibre, etc.

Hardwoods of Solihull,
Thornhill Road,
Solihull,
West Midlands.

Ebony and other hardwoods

Thomas Sutton Ltd,
37 Frederick Street
Birmingham 18.

Jewellers' and silversmiths' suppliers

Bales,
53 Hylton Street,
Birmingham 18.

Charles Cooper,
Hatton Garden,
London.

Frank Pike,
Hatton Garden,
London.

A. Shoot & Sons Ltd,
116 St John Street,
Clerkenwell,
London.

W. C. Bucknall Ltd,
83 Spencer Street,
Birmingham 18.

Electro-platers, gilders, bronzists

Fry's Metals,
Worcester Road
Kidderminster.

Tin alloys, pewter, and solders

Edward Day & Baker,
3 Vyse Street,
Birmingham 18.

Silver and silver solders

Englehard Industries Ltd
49 Spencer Street,
Birmingham 18,
Valley Road,
Cinderford,
Glos.

Johnson Matthey Ltd,
Vittoria Street,
Birmingham 18.

100 High Street,
Southgate,
London N14.

H. J. Edwards & Sons, 93 Barr Street, Birmingham 19.	*Brass and tin alloys*
J. Keatley (Metals) Ltd, 32A Shadwell Street, Birmingham 4.	
W. Gabb Ltd, 127 Barr Street, Birmingham 19.	
Peter Brine & Co. 20 Vyse Street, Birmingham 18.	*Brazing and hard solders for brass*
Hogg Laboratory Supplies, 125 Granville Street Birmingham 1.	*Chemicals and laboratory suppliers*
Philip Harris Ltd, Lynn Lane, Shenstone, Staffs.	
Hoben Davies Ltd, Spencroft Industrial Estate, Newcastle-under-Lyme, Staffs.	*Casting equipment*
F. Friedlein & Co. Ltd, 718 Old Ford Road, London E3.	*Ivory, mother of pearl, etc.*
The Assay Offices, Newhall Street, Birmingham 3.	*Information*
137 Portobello Street, Sheffield 14.	
15 Queen Street, Edinburgh.	
Goldsmiths' Hall, Gutter Lane, London.	
The Assay Office, Publications Dept, Goldsmiths Hall, Gutter Lane, London.	
Pewterer's Hall Lime Street, London.	
Hamish Bowie Ltd, 1696 High Street, Knowle, Warks.	*Metal testing solutions*

Bibliography

Abbey, S. *The Goldsmith's and Silversmith's Handbook* (Technical Press, 1968)
Bedford, John *Pewter* (Cassell, 1968)
Beedell, Suzanne *Restoring Junk* (Macdonald, 1970)
Blakemore, Kenneth *The Retail Jeweller's Guide* (Newnes-Butterworth, 1976)
Cotterell, Howard H. *Old Pewter, its Makers and Marks* (Batsford, 1968)
Cuzner, B. *A Silversmith's Manual* (N.A.G. Press, 1965)
Hughes, G. Bernard *Antique Sheffield Plate* (Batsford, 1970)
Macdonald-Taylor, M. *A Dictionary of Marks* (National Magazine Co, 1976)
Michaelis, Ronald F. *British Pewter* (Ward Lock, 1969)
Peal, Christopher A. *British Pewter and Britannia Metal* (John Gifford, 1971)
Taylor, Gerald *Silver* (Penguin, 1970)
Ullyett, Kenneth *Pewter: A Guide for Collectors* (Muller, 1973)

Materials for cover illustration supplied by
John Morch, Bishopsteignton, Devon.

Illustrated by Roger Day

British Library Cataloguing in Publication Data

Bowie, Hamish
  Renovating silver, pewter and brass. –
  (Penny pinchers).
  1. Metal-work – Conservation and
    restoration
  2. Silverware – Conservation and
    restoration
  3. Brasses – Conservation and restoration
  4. Pewter – Conservation and restoration
  I. Title   II. Series
  739'.14   NK6404.5

ISBN 0 7153 7871 6

Set in 9D on 11pt. Univers
and printed in Great Britain
by Redwood Burn Limited
Trowbridge & Esher
for David & Charles (Publishers) Limited
Brunel House Newton Abbot Devon